OUR
GR★AT
STATES

WHAT'S GREAT ABOUT

PENNSYLVANIA?

✹ By Kristin Marciniak

⌞ LERNER PUBLICATIONS COMPANY ✹ MINNEAPOLIS

CONTENTS

PENNSYLVANIA WELCOMES YOU! ✳ 4

Content Consultant: Paul C. Rosier, Professor and Chair of Department of History, Villanova University

Lerner Publications Company
A division of Lerner Publishing Group, Inc.
241 First Avenue North
Minneapolis, MN 55401 USA

For reading levels and more information, look up this title at www.lernerbooks.com.

Main body text set in ITC Franklin Gothic Std Book Condensed 12/15.
Typeface provided by Adobe Systems.

Library of Congress Cataloging-in-Publication Data

Marciniak, Kristin.
    What's great about Pennsylvania? / by Kristin Marciniak.
        pages cm. — (Our great states)
    Includes index.
    ISBN 978-1-4677-3334-2 (lib. bdg. : alk. paper)
      ISBN 978-1-4677-4717-2 (eBook)
      1. Pennsylvania—Juvenile literature. I. Title.
    F149.3.M27 2015
    974.8–dc23   2013049008

Manufactured in the United States of America
1 – PC – 7/15/14

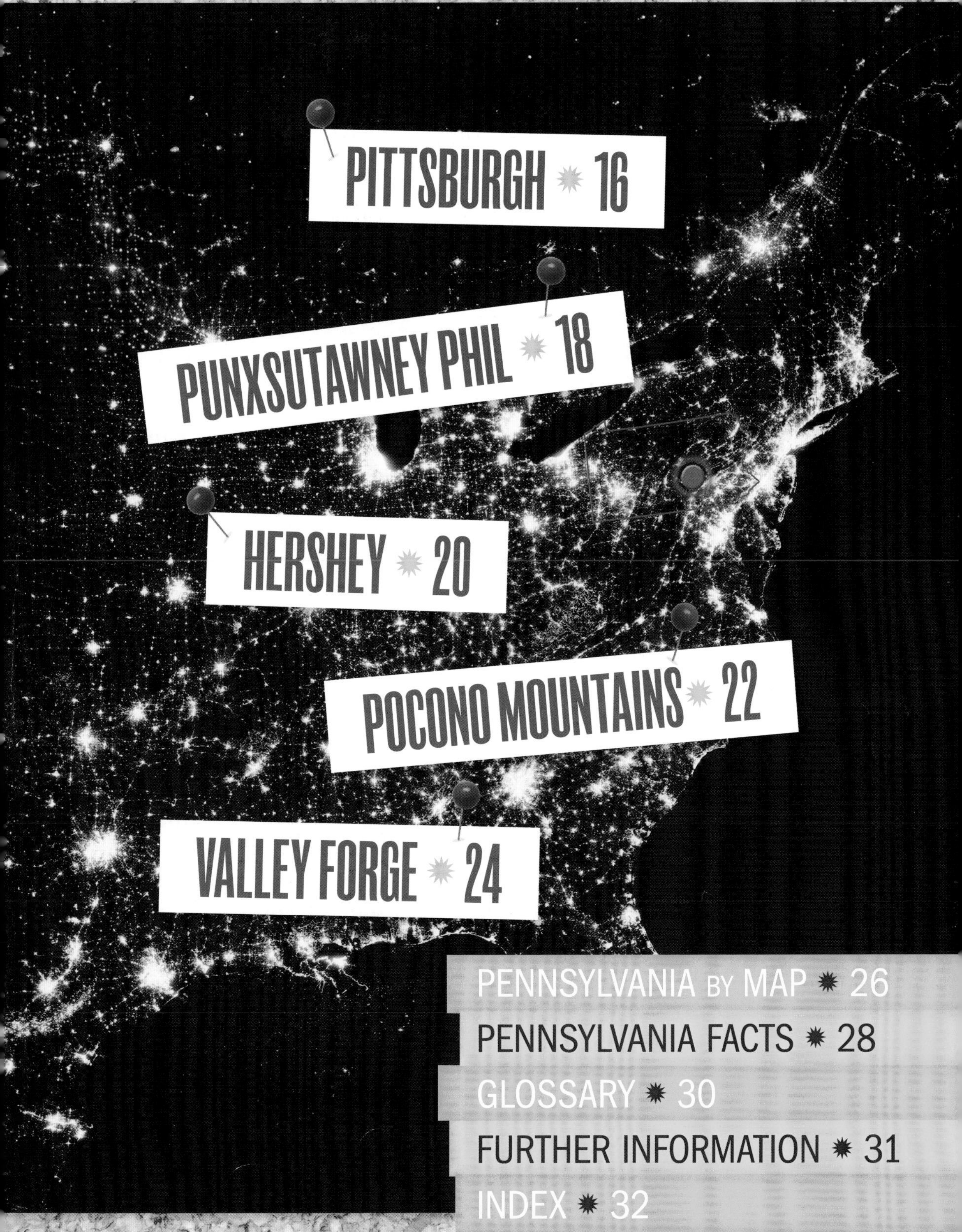

PENNSYLVANIA Welcomes You!

Pennsylvania has something for everyone! Philadelphia and Pittsburgh are known for historic locations and fun spots. Outside the cities in Dutch Country, you can see horse-drawn buggies sharing the road with cars. Or you can visit the Pocono Mountains for some hiking. You'll peek into the past at Gettysburg and Valley Forge. And don't forget to taste all the local foods! You won't want to miss the yummy soft pretzels. Pennsylvania has a lot to offer. Let's get started! Read on to discover ten things that make this state great. Welcome to Pennsylvania!

Pennsylvania
Welcomes You
STATE OF INDEPENDENCE

NEW YORK

OHIO

Erie

ALLEGHENY
PLATEAU

Allegheny River

A
P
P
A
L
A
C
H
I
A
N
M
O
U
N
T
A
I
N
S

Ohio River

Pittsburgh

Monongahela
River

Mount Davis
(3,213 ft/979 m)

WEST
VIRGINIA

MARYLAND

Susquehanna River

Miles
0   20   40

0   20   40   60
Kilometers

N

Scranton

POCONO
MOUNTAINS

Delaware River

Bethlehem
Allentown

NEW
JERSEY

Hershey

Reading

Harrisburg

Lancaster
County

Bensalem

Gettysburg

Upper Darby   Lower Merion

Philadelphia

DELAWARE

Explore Pennsylvania's
cities and all the places
in between! Just turn the
page to find out about the

KEYSTONE STATE. >

FABULOUS FOOD

> Start your trip to Pennsylvania with a snack. Philadelphia is famous for its cheesesteak sandwiches. Thinly sliced steak, fried onions, peppers, and cheese are served on a chewy roll. You can find these sandwiches in diners, food trucks, and fancy restaurants.

Philadelphia is also the birthplace of stromboli. This is pizza dough filled with cheese and pepperoni or sausage. The dough is baked until it is puffy and golden brown. You can enjoy it plain or with pizza sauce.

Breakfast fans should try scrapple. This is another dish from Philadelphia. Cornmeal and pork are mixed together. They are shaped into thin squares. The squares are fried and served hot. Scrapple is crispy on the outside and creamy on the inside.

Pennsylvania is also home to the pretzel. The Julius Sturgis Pretzel Bakery in Lancaster County was the United States' first pretzel bakery. It opened in 1861. The bakery still makes soft pretzels. You can even try twisting your own pretzels!

Bring your appetite when you visit. The delicious wonders of Pennsylvania are waiting for you.

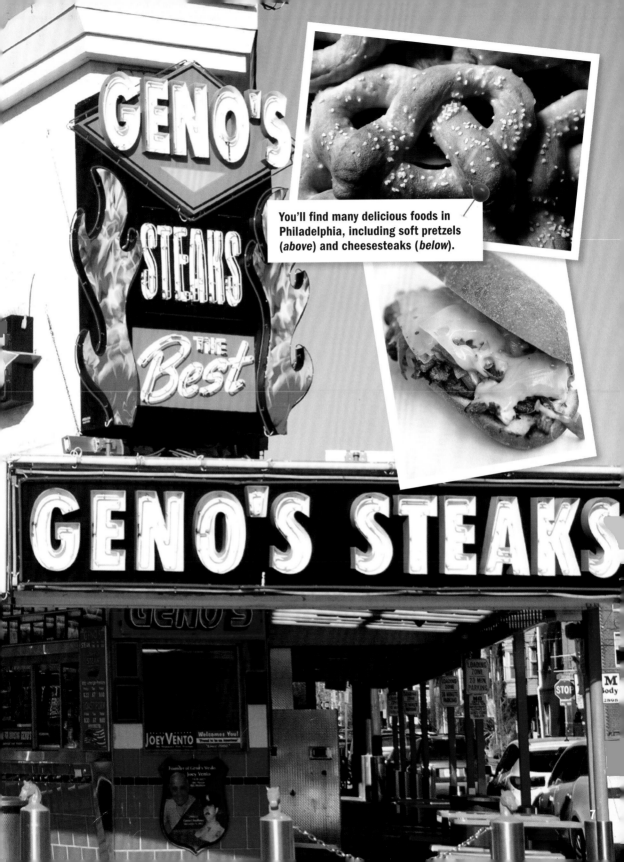

You'll find many delicious foods in Philadelphia, including soft pretzels (*above*) and cheesesteaks (*below*).

PHILADELPHIA

> Philadelphia is a city of firsts. It was one of the first cities in the United States. Now it is the largest city in Pennsylvania.

Take a step back in time and visit Franklin Court. This is where Benjamin Franklin's house used to be. Now you can explore the property. The Benjamin Franklin Museum is full of his inventions. Play with a computer edition of a glass harmonica.

Franklin started the University of Pennsylvania. It has the nation's first medical school. Make sure to check out the Penn Museum. The section on Egypt has a nearly 15-ton (14-metric-ton) sphinx!

The United States' first zoo is also in Philadelphia. The Philadelphia Zoo had 813 animals when it opened in 1874. Today it has 1,300 animals.

INDEPENDENCE HALL

Two of the most important papers in US history were prepared in Independence Hall in Philadelphia. The Declaration of Independence was written in 1776. The Constitution of the United States of America was written in 1787.

Benjamin Franklin was an important figure in Philadelphia in the 1700s.

LIBERTY BELL CENTER

> The Liberty Bell was first known as the State House Bell. It was made in 1751 to celebrate the fiftieth anniversary of Pennsylvania's constitution. The bell was later renamed the Liberty Bell. This is because the word *liberty* is carved on it.

The Liberty Bell developed a thin crack over the years. The crack grew even bigger when the bell rang on George Washington's birthday in 1846. The Liberty Bell has been silent ever since. You won't be able to hear it ring, but you can visit the bell. It is housed at the Liberty Bell Center in Philadelphia. This is just down the street from Independence Hall. Watch a short film on the history of the bell. Or check out the X-ray images of the bell and its crack. Read facts and myths about the bell. Make sure you observe the famous crack for yourself before you leave!

Although the Liberty Bell no longer rings, you can still see it on display.

The State House Bell used to ring in the 1700s and the 1800s.

LANCASTER COUNTY

> Life moves a little slower in Lancaster County. Maybe it is because of the open fields and fresh air. Or maybe it is the horse-drawn buggies.

This area of southern Pennsylvania is where German settlers lived in the 1700s. The Amish still live here. Life has not changed much for the Amish since the 1700s.

Many Amish communities do not use modern technology. They ride in buggies. Mules move farm machinery, and horses plow fields. Gas lanterns provide light at home.

Outsiders are curious about the Amish way of life. Learn more about Amish communities and how they live at the Amish Country Homestead. Then go on a tour of nearby farmlands. Finish the day with a meal in an Amish family's home.

While in Lancaster County, you can also visit the Strasburg Rail Road and the Railroad Museum of Pennsylvania. Explore old locomotives at the museum, or take a train ride through the countryside. Wave at the buggy drivers stopped at the railroad crossings!

THE AMISH

The Amish wear plain clothing. Men and boys wear dark suits and wide-brimmed hats. Women and girls wear long dresses with aprons. They speak Pennsylvania Deutsch at home. Children learn English in school. The Amish stop going to school after eighth grade.

People in Amish communities live simple lives. Most Amish families don't own cars.

GETTYSBURG

> The Battle of Gettysburg was one of the bloodiest battles of the Civil War (1861–1865). It happened from July 1 to July 3, 1863. Union soldiers from the North and Confederate soldiers from the South fought one another. The Union won, but it was not a happy victory. More than fifty thousand men died from both the North and the South.

Gettysburg is still best known for that battle. Tour the battlegrounds and the damaged buildings in town. Explore artifacts from the war at a tiny stone home. This home was Confederate general Robert E. Lee's headquarters. Make sure to visit the David Wills House. President Abraham Lincoln spent the night here before he gave his famous Gettysburg Address.

Gettysburg is also home to Gettysburg National Cemetery. US veterans from all major wars are buried here. Be sure to pay your respects to the soldiers. Learn more about the Civil War at the National Civil War Museum. It is forty-five minutes away in Harrisburg, the state capital.

THE GETTYSBURG ADDRESS

President Lincoln gave the Gettysburg Address four months after the battle. The speech was only a few minutes long. It is his most famous speech. It honored those who died. It also gave hope that the United States would one day be whole again.

This painting shows the bloody Battle of Gettysburg.

PITTSBURGH

> Pittsburgh used to be known for steel. Now it is known for arts, sports, and beautiful scenery. Start your visit at the Duquesne Incline. Take these wooden cable cars to the observation deck. See if you can spot the city and its three rivers. The Ohio River, the Monongahela River, and the Allegheny River are all visible.

Sports fans always have something to do in Pittsburgh. You can watch the Pittsburgh Pirates baseball team at PNC Park. Enjoy some peanuts as you cheer the team on. If you're visiting in the fall, stop by Heinz Field. You can watch a Pittsburgh Steelers football game. And from September through April, join hockey fans cheering for the Pittsburgh Penguins.

Art and history can be enjoyed year-round in Pittsburgh. See paintings from the 1800s and on at the Carnegie Museum of Art. Study the fossils on display at the Carnegie Museum of Natural History. Stop at the ToonSeum if you need a laugh. It is one of the only museums in the world about cartoons.

Be sure to bring good walking shoes. Pittsburgh is full of hills. It has 712 sets of outdoor staircases and nearly forty-five thousand steps. Getting from place to place can be a workout!

STEEL INDUSTRY

Steel was big in Pittsburgh from the 1870s to the early 1980s. It is made from iron heated by coal. Pennsylvania has a lot of iron and coal. It made sense to build steel factories in Pittsburgh. Not much steel is made in Pittsburgh these days. Many of the mills opened to help build factories during the Industrial Revolution. Steel is not in demand as it once was. But the city will always be known as Steel City.

Riding the Duquesne Incline will give you a good view of Pittsburgh.

PUNXSUTAWNEY PHIL

> Each year on February 2 in the city of Punxsutawney, people turn to someone who guesses when winter will end. This weatherman's name is Phil. Phil is a groundhog.

Thousands of people gather each year to see him pop out of his hole. Some people arrive as early as 3:00 a.m. Phil arrives around 7:00 a.m. You can expect six more weeks of winter if Phil sees his shadow on a sunny day. He gets scared by his shadow and goes back to his hole. Spring will come early if it is cloudy and there is no shadow.

If you're not in Punxsutawney on February 2, visit Phil at the library. This is where he lives year-round. You may even be able to have breakfast with Phil!

Phil is not actually good at guessing when winter will end. He is right less than half of the time. That's OK! February 2 is called Groundhog Day. It is fun to celebrate during the gloomiest part of winter.

Phil lives at the Punxsutawney
Memorial Library.

HERSHEY

> The first thing you will notice about the city of Hershey is the smell. It smells like delicious, rich chocolate. Make sure to look up as you walk the streets. The streetlights are shaped like foil-wrapped chocolate kisses. This might just be the sweetest place on Earth.

The town is named after Milton Hershey. He was a chocolate maker. Business was good in 1903. He decided to build a new factory in southern Pennsylvania. The workers did not have a place to live, so Milton also built a town.

Today Hershey is one of Pennsylvania's top tourist spots. You can see how chocolate is made at Hershey's Chocolate World. Try making candy in the Chocolate Lab. And be sure to save plenty of room for the samples of chocolate at the end.

When you have had your fill of sweets, check out the Hershey Museum. It is filled with facts and artifacts from Milton's life.

The most popular area in Hershey is Hershey Park. It was built in 1907 as an amusement park for local families to relax and play. It has eleven roller coasters and dozens of other rides for thrill seekers.

Milton Hershey (*right*) built the town of Hershey as the home for his growing chocolate company.

POCONO MOUNTAINS

> The Pocono Mountains are part of the Allegheny Plateau in the Appalachian Mountains. There is no better place to enjoy the beauty of Pennsylvania.

The Pocono Mountains region covers 2,400 square miles (6,216 square kilometers). It has nine state parks and two national parks. There are 170 miles (274 km) of rivers and 163 ski trails.

The most famous Poconos area is the Delaware Water Gap. The land here was once a flat plain. The Delaware River wore down the rock over thousands of years. A gorge formed. It is a great place for hiking and canoeing.

Hikers should also head over to Bushkill Falls. There are eight waterfalls connected by trails. The highest and most amazing is Main Falls. It is 300 feet (91 meters).

Make sure to stop at the No. 9 Coal Mine and Museum in Lansford. This coal mine was used from 1855 to 1972. The underground tour features the miner's hospital and the original elevator shaft.

There is no shortage of animals and scenery to see in the Poconos region.

VALLEY FORGE

> No battles were fought at Valley Forge. Still, some say it is where the Revolutionary War (1775–1783) was won.

George Washington and his troops lived at Valley Forge during the winter of 1777 to 1778. It was a hard winter. Two thousand of the twelve thousand soldiers died from hunger, disease, and the cold. The rest spent their days training for battle. The training paid off. The Continental Army, which Washington led, went on to win the Revolutionary War.

Valley Forge is now a national historic park. Explore copies of the log huts built by the soldiers. Or tour the Isaac Potts House, where Washington spent most of his time. Learn what camp life was like from the costumed actors that walk the grounds. Can you imagine spending a winter here?

Valley Forge is a great place for nature lovers. Hike, bike, or ride horses on one of the many trails in the park. Look out for really fast runners. Some people use Valley Forge as a training ground for the Olympics.

YOUR TOP TEN!

You have read about ten awesome things to do and see in Pennsylvania. What would your Pennsylvania top ten list include? What would you like to see and do if you visited Pennsylvania? What attraction has you the most excited? These are all things to think about as you write down your own top tens. Make your top ten list on a separate sheet of paper. Turn your list into a book. Illustrate it with drawings or pictures from the Internet or magazines.

This statue of George Washington can be seen at Valley Forge.

The winter of 1777–1778 was hard on the Continental Army.

PENNSYLVANIA BY MAP

Erie

> ## MAP KEY

⭐ Capital city

◯ City

◯ Point of interest

▲ Highest elevation

—·— State border

----- County border

OHIO

N

ALLEGHENY PLATEAU

Allegheny River

Ohio River

Punxsutawney Phil
(Punxsutawney)

APPALACHIAN

Pittsburgh

Duquesne Incline
Carnegie Museum of Art
ToonSeum

Monongahela River

Mount Davis
(3,213 ft/979 m)

WEST VIRGINIA

Visit www.lerneresource.com
to learn more about the state
flag of Pennsylvania.

VIRTUE LIBERTY AND INDEPENDENCE

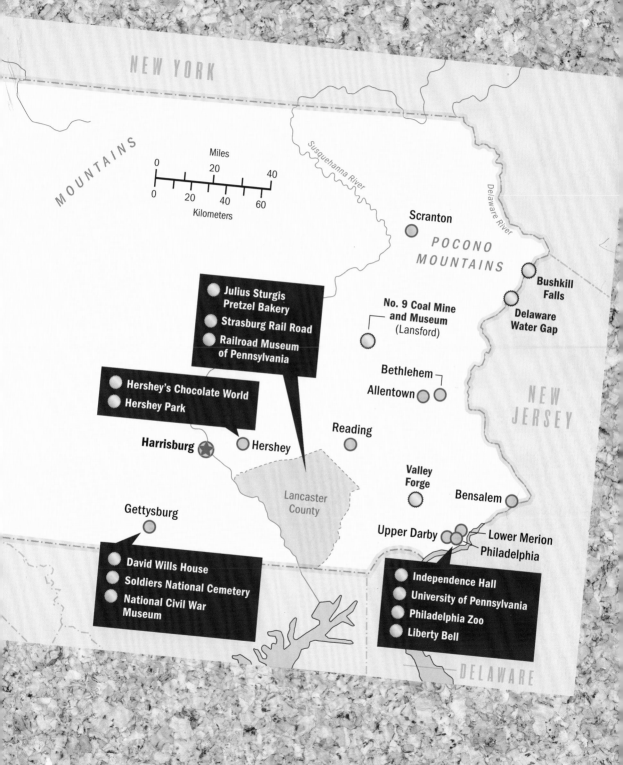

NEW YORK

MOUNTAINS

Miles
0   20   40
0   20   40   60
Kilometers

Susquehanna River

Delaware River

Scranton

POCONO
MOUNTAINS

Bushkill
Falls

Delaware
Water Gap

Julius Sturgis
Pretzel Bakery
Strasburg Rail Road
Railroad Museum
of Pennsylvania

No. 9 Coal Mine
and Museum
(Lansford)

Bethlehem

Allentown

NEW
JERSEY

Hershey's Chocolate World
Hershey Park

Reading

Harrisburg   Hershey

Valley
Forge

Bensalem

Lancaster
County

Upper Darby

Lower Merion
Philadelphia

Gettysburg

David Wills House
Soldiers National Cemetery
National Civil War
Museum

Independence Hall
University of Pennsylvania
Philadelphia Zoo
Liberty Bell

DELAWARE

PENNSYLVANIA FACTS

NICKNAME: Keystone State

SONG: "Pennsylvania" by Eddie Khoury and Ronnie Bonner

MOTTO: "Virtue, Liberty, and Independence"

FLOWER: mountain laurel

TREE: hemlock

BIRD: ruffed grouse

ANIMAL: whitetail deer

FOOD: milk

DATE AND RANK OF STATEHOOD: December 12, 1787; the 2nd state

CAPITAL: Harrisburg

AREA: 44,742 square miles (115,881 sq. km)

AVERAGE JANUARY TEMPERATURE: 26.5°F (-3°C)

AVERAGE JULY TEMPERATURE: 71.4°F (22°C)

POPULATION AND RANK: 12,763,536; 6th (2012)

MAJOR CITIES AND POPULATIONS: Philadelphia (1,526,006), Pittsburgh (305,704), Allentown (118,032), Erie (101,786), Reading (88,082), Upper Darby (82,795)

NUMBER OF US CONGRESS MEMBERS: 18 representatives, 2 senators

NUMBER OF ELECTORAL VOTES: 20

NATURAL RESOURCES: coal, petroleum, natural gas, iron ore, lead, zinc, granite, clay

AGRICULTURAL PRODUCTS: dairy, apples, peaches, cherries, grapes

MANUFACTURED GOODS: clothing, textiles, chemicals, pharmaceuticals

STATE HOLIDAYS AND CELEBRATIONS: Groundhog Day, Gettysburg Festival

GLOSSARY

Amish: a religious group whose members settled in the United States in the 1700s and continue to live in a traditional way on farms

artifact: a typically simple object that shows human work and represents a culture

attraction: something interesting or enjoyable that people want to visit, see, or do

constitution: the system of beliefs and laws by which a country, state, or organization is governed

food truck: a large vehicle equipped with facilities for cooking and selling food

glass harmonica: a musical instrument with rotating glass bowls of differing sizes played by touching the dampened edges with a finger

gorge: a narrow passage, ravine, or steep-walled canyon

plateau: a broad flat area of high land

shaft: a vertical opening through the floors of a building

LERNER

SOURCE

Expand learning beyond the printed book. Download free, complementary educational resources for this book from our website, www.lerneresource.com.

FURTHER INFORMATION

Burford, Betty. *Chocolate by Hershey: A Story about Milton S. Hershey.* Minneapolis: Millbrook Press, 1994. Follow Milton Hershey from his days as an ice-cream scooper to his huge success as a chocolatier.

Civil War Trust
http://www.civilwar.org/battlefields/gettysburg/assets/ten-facts-about/ten-facts-about-gettysburg.html
Take a closer look at the bloodiest battle in US history and learn a few more facts before you visit this historic ground.

Figley, Marty Rhodes. *Who Was William Penn? And Other Questions about the Founding of Pennsylvania.* Minneapolis: Lerner Publications, 2012. Learn all about the early days of Pennsylvania and how it played an important role in the formation of the United States.

Jerome, Kate Boehm. *Pennsylvania: What's So Great about This State?* Charleston, SC: Arcadia Publishing, 2011. Find out why Pennsylvania is known as the birthplace of the nation and more in this fun, fact-filled book.

The Official Tourism Website of the State of Pennsylvania
http://www.visitpa.com
Explore all there is to do, see, and learn in our nation's second state.

Pennsylvania History
http://www.history.com/topics/us-states/pennsylvania
This site contains a rundown of the basic facts about Pennsylvania, as well as important people, dates, and events.

INDEX

PHOTO ACKNOWLEDGMENTS

The images in this book are used with the permission of: © Songquan Deng/iStockphoto, p. 1; © benkrut/iStockphoto, p. 4; © Laura Westlund/Independent Picture Service, pp. 5 (top), 26–27; © Snehitdesign/iStockphoto, 5 (bottom); © travelif/iStockphoto, pp. 6–7; © AwakenedEye/iStockphoto, p. (7 (top); © Hwang, Kent/The Food Passionates/Corbis, p. 7 (bottom); © KenKPhoto/iStockphoto, pp. 8–9; © Leif Skoogfors/Corbis, p. 8; Library of Congress, pp. 9 (LC-USZC4-7214), 11 (bottom) (LC-USZ62-821), 14 (LC-DIG-ppmsca-19305), 15 (LC-USZC4-2088), 16 (LC-USF34-043202-D), 25 (left) (LC-USZ62-819); © stanley45/iStockphoto, pp. 10–11; © Richard T. Nowitz/Corbis, pp. 11 (top), 23 (left), 24–25; © Victor Pelaez/iStockphoto, pp. 12–13; © photopia/iStockphoto, p. 12; © Glowimages/Corbis, p. 13; © Pittsburgh Post-Gazette/ZUMA Press/Corbis, pp. 14–15; © Richard Cummins/Corbis, pp. 16–17; © pcharlesfisher/iStockphoto, p. 17; © David Maxwell/epa/Corbis, pp. 18–19; © Alan Freed/Shutterstock Images, p. 19; © Lissandra Melo/Shutterstock Images, pp. 20–21; © Richard T. Nowitz/Corbis, p. 21 (left); © Hershey Community Archives, p. 21 (right); © Songquan Deng/iStockphoto, pp. 22–23; © sigenest/iStockphoto, p. 23 (right); © Delmas Lehman/iStockphoto, p. 25 (right); © nicoolay/iStockphoto, p. 26; © Jteate/iStockphoto, p. 29 (top); © twildlife/iStockphoto, p. 29 (middle top); © Dobresum/iStockphoto, p. 29 (middle bottom); © npage/iStockphoto, p. 29 (bottom).

Front cover: Cover: © iStockphoto.com/rabbit75_ist (Pocono Mountains); © iStockphoto.com/LadyVictoria (Strasburg Railroad); © Tetra images/Thinkstock (Liberty Bell); Carol M. Highsmith Archive, Library of Congress LC-DIG-highsm-14695 (Amish); © Laura Westlund/Independent Picture Service (map); © iStockphoto.com/fpm (seal); © iStockphoto.com/vicm (pushpins); © iStockphoto.com/benz190 (cork board).